Hampden
EXIT 9A
Cafe Hon

My year as

BALTIMORE'S BEST HON

by

Charlene E. Osborne

Principal photographer David Muse

Hon Cave Press, LLC
Baltimore, Maryland

Hon Cave Press, LLC
P.O. Box 5274
Highlandtown, Maryland 21224-9998
www.honcavepress.com

ISBN: 978-0-9845404-0-2
Printing by Four Colour Print Group
Printed in Korea by Tara TPS Co., Ltd
Design by Middleton Evans
Proofreading by David and Kathryn Muse
Graphic production by Elizabeth Davidson

Best Hon 2009

Dedication

To my Mom - Doreen, Dad - Charles and Brother - Dorman.

Every day, I want to call you, to share my day or ask about yours. I want to ask for your advice, guidance or memories. "Mom, how do I paint this screen?" "Dad, how do I fix this door?", " Dorm, do you remember when we were kids and how mom used to call us to dinner with that blaring police whistle?" Everyone in the neighborhood knew when the Osborne kids were summoned home.

I feel your presence so greatly that I forget, all of you are no longer here. I may no longer be able to reach you by phone but am comforted knowing I can reach into my heart and see you, feel you and continue to love you with my whole heart and soul. I thank God and you for watching over me, guiding me, protecting me. I am blessed.

To all the Baltimore Hons, past, present and future.

I would also like to dedicate this to all of our United States service men and women fighting to protect us. God Bless all of them and keep them safe.

Life is short, so have some fun, Hon.

Charlene Osborne

FEB 59

HONFEST
2009

Foreword

We here in Baltimore know that hon is a term of endearment, short for honey. Use of the word hon is wide-spread throughout the Baltimore neighborhoods of Dundalk, Essex, Hampden, and Highlandtown. The word is a way of being civil and polite, yet homespun and informal all at once. In essence, the use of hon is a way to draw closer to those one meets. If you capitalize the word, Hon refers to a woman.

With her poem about a Dundalk girl feeling blessed, Charlene Osborne won the title of Bawlmer's Best HON 2009. Not one to rest on her laurels, or rhinestone tiara to be precise, she decided to make the most of her year-long reign. She used her fame and renown to give back to the community. Her appearance at various events benefited such charities as the Johns Hopkins Children Center and the Maryland Special Olympics; boosted support for such community organizations as the Baltimore Art & Music Project and the Dundalk Renaissance Corporation; and drew attention to a variety of local small businesses. In general, as Bawlmer's Best HON 2009 Charlene served as emissary of the good will and all the charm that Charm City Baltimore has to offer.

I have had the distinct pleasure of photographing Charlene on many of her hon-derful adventures. It has been heart-warming to witness the joyful reactions of most people she meets, be they young children at a parade or senior citizens in a retirement home. It has been hilarious to watch the double-takes and curious side-long glances those unfamiliar with the Bawlmer hon tradition give to Charlene. And, it has been a true joy to meet a number of the women who preceded Charlene as Bawlmer's Best HON, in particular Heidi and Rita Moore.

This book, My Year as Baltimore's Best HON, allows you a glimpse inside the hive of beehive hairdo life. Marvel at the ever-present colorful outfits, blue eye shadow, and lots of hairspray (by the way, you do know that the higher one's hair, the closer one is to heaven, right?). Join the fun and excitement of a once-in-a-lifetime visit inside the secret Hon-cave. Accompany Charlene and her hon-derful friends on a sedate (that's what she says!) night out on the town or on a weekend trip down the ocean. Rock along to the music of bands of renown and discover that the King (well, at least his many admirers) is indeed still in the house. Join her backstage at the theater, onstage at the Polar Bear Plunge, and out and about in a neighborhood near you.

I have enjoyed an uproarious and fun-filled adventure following Charlene during her reign. Now that your travels with Bawlmer's Best HON 2009 are about to begin, I trust it will be equally wild and rewarding.

My Year as Baltimore's Best HON celebrates the warm and generous spirit of Charlene Osborne, Bawlmer's Best HON 2009. She draws us closer together. It is we who are blessed to know Charlene.

To this daughter of Dundalk and Baltimore, I say thanks and best wishes for continued success. You are a real cutie-patootie, hon!

-David Muse

Introduction

Once upon a time in a little community on the eastern outskirts of Dundalk, Maryland, a little Hon-flower was sprouting. It was the early 1960's, and no one knew at the time that she would blossom into Baltimore's Best HON, but the signs were there.

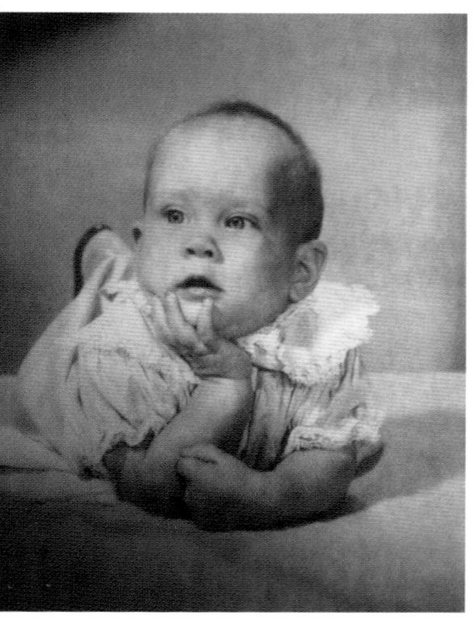

Welcome to my Hon-derful life. Occasionally I am asked, by those not from Baltimore or those simply too young to know: "What does the word, Hon, mean? What is a Hon? How can I become a Hon?" I hope the following pages will answer some of your questions and give you a glimpse inside this Hon-derful world.

Anyone, woman or man, can be a hon. Just be kind, be yourself, and have a unique Baltimore retro sense of style. It helps if you can speak Baltimorese.

My Hon-derful life began while growing up in Dundalk, Maryland. Dundalk was founded in 1894 by William McShane, the son of Henry McShane, whose company the McShane Bell Foundry crafted brass bells. Some you could ring in your hand, and others weighed over 10,000 pounds. William McShane bought land formerly know as the St. Helena area and renamed it in honor of Dundalk, Ireland, his father's birthplace. Dundalk, Maryland has grown and prospered for more than 100 years. McShane Bells are well-known and are found throughout the United States.

I attended Edgemere Elementary School and General John Stricker Jr. High School. After graduation from Patapsco Sr. High School, I studied whatever my hon heart desired: real estate, interior design, acting, bar tending, CADD, screenwriting, and civil engineering. This led me into the field of transportation design, a career I have enjoyed for the past 12 years with the same company right here in Baltimore.

I grew up with the Baltimore dialect in Dundalk, where it is still prevalent today. I am somehow comforted when I hear: "Hi Hon, how you'se doin today? What can I gitcha ta eat Hon?" My answer ... "steamed crabs and a Natty Boh please". I'm not so comforted when I hear: "Good afternoon, ma'am. What will you be dining on this afternoon?" My answer ... "the table?"

The Baltimore accent is a legitimate dialect often referred to as Baltimorese. It originated among the white, blue-collar workers in Baltimore City and surrounding eastern counties. It is said that the accent is largely southern-sounding, mixed with a Philadelphia accent. Baltimore's Best HONs speak Baltimorese fluently. The best way to learn the dialect is to conduct an Internet search on Baltimore dialect. You will find a plethora of sites dedicated to the history, spelling, and pronunciation of the words. For example, I was born in Dundock, Merlin of the Unighted States of Merika. I like to go downy oshin and swim in da wooder. After I eat dem steamed crabs, I warsh my hands in da zink next to the turlit. I like to get flars and jewrie on my birfday, hon. Most of you will have fun learning, and some of you may be able to contribute a few new words to the many lists. It's all fun, Hon!

Fast forward to the year 2004. I was visiting Hollywood, California with a friend. As we strolled down Hollywood Boulevard, I vividly remember stopping dead in my tracks in front of this amazing store. My jaw dropped, and my eyes were wide as saucers. I was mesmerized by the colors and great heights of these fantastic sculptures. These were not just wigs; they were true works of art. Once inside, I ran from one wig to the next proclaiming "I have to have this one and this one and this one!" Then reality set in, and I realized I had no money to buy the contents of this store. I was lucky to have saved enough to pay the tolls to get home. Finally, I breathed into a paper bag to calm my hyperventilation and decided to purchase just two wigs. The first one I had to have because it screamed BALTIMORE and John Waters. I once had an extra part in his movie Serial Mom and have been a fan of his ever since. The first wig was a beautifully coiffed blonde beehive, nearly a foot high. The second wig was a bit more theatrical with its enormous bouffant height, neon red hair, and yellow accents. It looked like a giant inferno, so I named it Blaze. I did not know why I wanted this wig or where I would wear it. I just knew I had to have it. You could say the rest is history.

In the spring of 2005, I read an article about an upcoming festival called HonFest. I looked at the fun, colorful photos and knew I wanted to participate. This was the opportunity I had been waiting for! I researched HonFest and its history. I learned that Denise Whiting, owner of Café HON in Hampden, started the festival in the early 1990's as a costume contest. It now is a festive weekend event which celebrates the unique life and style of Baltimore women from the 1950's and 1960's. This annual summer tradition takes place on the Avenue (36th Street) in Hampden, Maryland. It has grown into an internationally known festival that spans four city blocks lined with quirky shops and eclectic restaurants. HonFest is recognized as the largest festival of its kind drawing nearly sixty thousand people during the two day event.

In my quest for ideas on what to wear, I researched famous Baltimore women from the 1950's and 1960's. One woman in particular stood out. Her style was elegant. Her feather boa was decadent. And, her hair was blazing red. It was the amazingly beautiful and wildly successful exotic entertainer Blaze Starr. Now that I had my inspiration, I began working feverishly on my artistic interpretation of this stunning Baltimore icon. My friends said I appeared to be possessed by Edward Scissorhands. My home was covered in shredded fabric and plastic. I had a few nips and cuts to bear, but the costume was ready. To top it all off, I finally had a purpose for my enormous wig named Blaze. When dressed, I felt glamorous and retro. Keep in mind that I work at an engineering design job all day and have never been an exotic entertainer. Unless you consider the few years in the early 1980's when I tended bar at the world famous Hammerjacks.

My inner and outer hon was now ready for HonFest. With my platform boots, blazing red hair, and outstretched arm holding a gigantic parasol, I was nearly fourteen feet high. I towered into the festival, and my best friends Leslie and Gina tended to me like bridesmaids. They made sure I did not electrocute myself on the overhead power lines or burst into flames when the streamers accidentally blew across the open flame grills of the food vendors. We decided it would be much safer if I stood in one open location. Once we stopped, lines of people began to form. That day, I held more babies than a politician. My legs were like jelly from kneeling to pose with children. I did not know what to expect and was overwhelmed by the request for photos and hugs. Some of the locals made the connection to Blaze Starr and, at that moment, I became Blaze Char – the Baltimore Hon.

Later that day, I competed in the Baltimore's Best HON contest and was not as successful with the judges as I was with the crowd. I went home, soaked my bleeding, blistered feet and exhausted body in the tub and cried while I reflected on the events of the day. I was not crying because I lost the contest. I cried because it was one of the most unusual and rewarding days of my life. I have yet to learn how to put the experience into words.

Family priorities prevented me from attending HonFest in 2006 and 2007. The week before HonFest 2008 I hand-painted a window screen, a folk art unique to Baltimore. I planned to go to the festival in 2008 only to direct and film a commercial I wrote for a Klondike Ice Cream video contest. After the shoot wrapped, I realized there was still time to dress up and enter the contest. I donned the sky-high blonde beehive from LA, the painted window screen top (to use along with a poem I wrote for the talent portion of the competition), flaming pink flamingo capri pants, and a newly created parasol. I believed I had little chance of winning Baltimore's Best Hon because my beehive was a wig. After I lost in 2005, someone mentioned to me that you must use your real hair to be able to win. In 2008, a thyroid issue caused me to loose a lot of my hair for a few months. I decided not to put my own hair – that had finally grown back – through the rigors of a beehive hairdo. I had a magnificently sculpted beehive wig that had been sitting on a shelf for the past four years so I decided to wear it with pride; even if it meant no chance of winning.

There were sixty contestants vying for Baltimore's Best HON. When it was my turn on stage, I delivered my poem in my best Baltimorese and displayed my painted window screen top. In the end I was out Hon-ned by 77 year-young Agnes "Punkin" Hurly, the winner of HonFest 2008. Second place went to the lovely lady in leopard print, Sandy Puhl. I was shocked to still be standing in the top three and Hon-ored to lose to my favorite Hon "Punkin."

In spring 2009, I was busy creating my HonFest costume. I decided this would be my final competition. I would again don my blonde beehive but wanted to do something very special. I hand painted my entire outfit and created a window screen for my skirt. My ensemble made me look like a giant pink flamingo from front and back. After seeing this final outfit, I was inspired to write another poem. Technically, it's a really long limerick, but whose judging.

My painted window screen outfit, heartfelt poem (limerick, I guess), and a little bit of genuine Hon personality were the winning combination on June 14, 2009. I humbly accepted the trophy and the title of Baltimore's Best HON. I now proudly wear the tiara and sash as Bawlmer's Best HON 2009!

As the winner of HonFest 2009, Denise Whiting invited me to attend two official events. First there was the fantastic and over the top Night of 100 Elvises, a benefit for John's Hopkins Children Center. Denise gathered a group of friends and past BBH winners and treated us to a very special night out. Elvis and the Hons go together like peanut butter and bananas – fantastic! Next was the Baltimore Mayor's Christmas Parade through Hampden. I was invited to ride on a convertible next to Denise and was honored to wish everyone a Happy Holiday, Hon!

A number of extraordinary events arose during this year and created opportunities for me to appear as Bawlmer's Best HON 2009. When a battle brewed between City Hall and Denise Whiting over the giant pink flamingo that adorned the front of Cafe Hon, Denise invited the Hons to rally alongside her. Baltimore's very own 98 Rock radio station, including well-known station celebrities Mickey, Amelia, and Spiegel, gave new meaning to having your back for a good cause. In the wee hours of the morning,

98 Rock appeared and placed 1000 pink flamingo lawn ornaments on the lawn in front of City Hall. The message was loud and clear. Leave the pink flamingo, a Baltimore icon, alone! After the successful meeting between Mayor Shelia Dixon and Denise, I celebrated by dancing among the 1000 flamingos. It was a very Mary Tyler Moore moment and just plain fun, hon!

At each of my early public appearances, I would receive invitations to attend other events as the Hon. Because my reign as Bawlmer's Best HON was only for one year, I decided to accept each invitation, especially if it were for a good cause. I wanted to make the most and best use of this year and would include as many of my friends that enthusiastically wanted to participate. I started to collect photos for a yearbook documenting my experience. After requesting photos from photographers I had met over the years and during this hon-derful journey, I was blessed when some of Baltimore and DC's best photographers agreed to help me document this rare and exciting opportunity. They are an amazing DREAM TEAM of talent and very special people. It's one thing to photograph Hons at HonFest; it's a whole different animal to capture Hons on film in the wild. You are about to see this incredible Dream Team's talent brilliantly poured out on the pages of this book.

Allow me to introduce my Dream Team to you: the talented and dedicated photography of David Muse, Principal Photographer; the spectacular and Hon-derful photography of the lovely Jaime Windon; and, the Heaven-sent guidance and images of master photographer Middleton Evans.

The Legendary Blaze Starr

(birth name: Fannie Belle Fleming)

When I needed vintage inspiration for my 2005 HonFest costume, my research for iconic Baltimore women of the 1950s led me to a fiery redhead named Blaze Starr. This photo was all the inspiration I needed.

In 1983, Blaze Starr retired from the entertainment industry as an actress and queen of burlesque. In 1989, she became a gemologist. Recently, I was excited to learn she was still busy creating her beautiful and exotic jewelry. To my surprise, she autographed the inside lid of each box of jewelry I purchased, and she included this legendary photo of herself. I was honored when she gave me her blessing to use the nickname Blaze Char.

"Charlene"
Congratulations
on
Winning
"Honfest"
Blaze
Starr

BLAZE CHAR

Arriving at HonFest 2005 in this over the top artistic interpretation of Blaze Starr, I met Denise Whiting for the first time. She wasn't quite sure what to make of me but was very pleasant. I was not quite sure what to expect at the festival, but it turned out to be one of the most magical days I have ever experienced.

HON

ART FOR HON SAKE

During HonFest you will find hon-tastic works of art displayed throughout the neighborhood of Hampden. There is a newly created art competition that draws many interesting entries, including this winning creation (left) by Holly Petr.

PUNKIN'S BIG DAY

HonFest 2008 drew a record number of entrants. Sixty competitors vied for Baltimore's Best Hon, but in the end Contestant 9, the adorable Agnes "Punkin" Hurley (below) became Number 1. Denise

HonFest,

a poem by Charlene Osborne

Roses is Red.
Violets is Blue.

Highlandtown's where Hons come from
and Dundalk is too.

East Bawlmer blooms Hons
Like spring time does flowers.

Thank God for Hampden
for making HonFest ours!

Whiting held the microphone steady as I nervously introduced myself (top right). My hand-painted window screen attached to my top, pink parasol, and poem (spoken in my best Baltimorese) secured me a 3rd place win behind the lovely Sandy Puhl (below left).

Bawlmer's Best Hon
HONFEST
2009

And The Winner Is

BLESSED,

a poem by Charlene Osborne

There once was a Hon from Dundalk.
They said she spoke real funny Bawlmer talk.
She looked like a flamingo,
And kept hollerin', "BINGO"!
And her beehive was high as a beanstalk.

Well, she went to Hampden one day.
And had lunch in this little café.
They said..."WELCOME TO CAFE' HON"
"You're gonna have some fun,"
and she enjoyed the perfect day.

She realized she didn't need a Mercedes Benz,
Or have to follow the current trends.
She and her beehive
had finally arrived
And was now surrounded by lots of friends.

So she decided to come to HonFest.
And compete amongst the very best.
Win or Lose...
She won't have the blues,
Because she truly feels blessed.

7

STIFF COMPETITION

As the three judges, Judge Judy (Denise's Mom), Judge Janet and Judge Elliana (below) sat in the sweltering June heat, the contestants strolled out one by one and showcased their talent or spoke in Baltimorese to impress them. I was honored just to be included in the top ten of these hon-tastic ladies who truly embody the hon spirit. Dress included everything from muumuus and curlers to leopard print spandex, complemented by the classic cat-eye glasses. It was a tall challenge, but the tiara finally adorned my beehive.

Bawlmer's Best Hon

Hons Gone Wild

At most pageants, the awarding of the winner's sash is a pretty routine affair. Not so for the Bawlmer's Best Hon competition at the 15th annual HonFest in Hampden. To begin with, Charlene Osborne, who beat out nine semifinalists, including an American flag-themed Hon, a knitting-needle Hon, and a gold lamé Hon, is almost six feet tall. Add two feet of blonde beehive and you have a genuine logistical dilemma.

The 2008 winner, Agnes "Punkin'" Hurley, sporting hair curlers and a housedress, officially presented the prize, after describing her reign as "the best time I've had in my 77 years, toolin' all 'round Bawlmer." But alas, at little more than five feet tall, Hurley was helpless in getting the hot pink sash over Osborne's mountain of hair and Aquanet.

Ultimately, Café Hon owner and HonFest creator Denise Whiting was able to secure the sash, which matched Osborne's elbow-length gloves and the flamingo printed on her skirt. She also presented the winner with tickets for a cruise, a case of Pompeian olive "ool," and a vintage suitcase with a "B'lieve, Hon" bumper sticker.

After the presentation, the house band resumed playing local standards like "I Fell in Love with a Baltimore Hon," and attention turned to Pompeian's duckpin bowling tent and the further devouring of the Guinness-certified "World's Biggest Crabcake," being doled out in sandwich-sized portions for $5.50 a pop by servers in multi-clawed crab hats.

Soon, all eyes turned to the dunking booth where Whiting, having changed into an old-fashioned lime green bathing suit covered with sequins, was ready to get wet to raise money for Maryland Special Olympics. Her cat-eye glasses, needless to stay, stayed on the entire time.

–Jamie McCoy for Baltimore Magazine, edited by Evan Serpick

Bawlmer's Best Hon 2009

A MOST MEMORABLE 4th OF JULY

When my hometown got wind that a local Hon brought the trophy and the title of Baltimore's Best Hon home to Dundalk, they rolled out the red carpet and gave me a warm welcome.

One of my most memorable experiences this year had to be walking in the 75th annual Fourth of July Dundalk Heritage Parade. While the band The Martians rocked the crowd (above), hundreds of parade marchers, including me in my hand-painted window screen portrait of Abraham Lincoln, followed in line. Though grateful for the offer to ride in the *All Stretched Out* Hummer limousine, I preferred to walk behind the car, which gave me the honor to talk to everyone along the parade route. A decision I will never forget or regret. A tall handsome gentleman stepped into the street stopping the parade. With his arm around my shoulder, he asked "Do you know who I am?" I said "Yes sir, you are Mr. Woods." We gave each other a big hug. He asked "What are you doing now?" and I replied, "I work in engineering / transportation design." With a huge smile he said "It was the math" and I said, "No sir, it was the math teacher." The parade began to move. He dashed back into the crowd before I had a chance to say "Thank you Mr. Woods for being the best math teacher a 7th and 8th grade student could ever wish for."

GREAT BALLS OF FIRE

Duckpin bowling began in Baltimore around 1900 and is still played today. The sport got its name because when the ball hit the pins, they wildly flew about and looked like a flock of ducks. Walking into the Edgemere Bowl in Edgemere, Maryland is like walking back in time. For a fun Hon night out, my friends and I decided to dress vintage and celebrate the sport. Calling ourselves, Team Hon and the Greasers (right), we rocked the lanes. The Hons cheered on Zach Stack (below) as he bowled for a strike.

TRICK OR TREAT

Each October, the Creative Alliance at The Patterson in Baltimore City brings us a world-renowned paper lantern spectacular. When the sun sets, 1200 paper lanterns begin to glow and magically move along the pathways of Patterson Park. Intermingled among the stilt walkers and the Bone Band, hundreds of costumed families march along at this annual glowing tradition – The Great Halloween Lantern Parade.

BIRDS OF A FEATHER ...

Orioles
PROUD TO BE YOUR
HOMETOW TEAM!
Thank You
For Your Donation
To Benefit
Haitian Relief

FLOCK TOGETHER

Baltimore's famous sports teams take on an avian theme. All the more reason that a flamingo-loving Hon would support her other favorite birds, the Baltimore Ravens and the Baltimore Orioles. While attending a Ravens game, I took the opportunity to help raise awareness for the Maryland State Police and Special Olympics Polar Bear Plunge by supporting team Plunging Hons. Never a dull moment at a Ravens tailgate especially when joined by friends and the famous fan The Bird Man of Baltimore (following page top).

O's

STEELERS
RAVENS
PLUNGING
HONS.com

THE HIGHER THE HAIR,
THE BIGGER THE WIN. GO RAVENS!

BIRD TOWN

The lawn of Baltimore City Hall never looked so good. A public flocking was issued to Mayor Sheila Dixon and City Officials by Mickey, Amelia, and Spiegel of 98 Rock on behalf of Denise Whiting and the iconic pink flamingo sculpture. The flamingo aka Big Pink had peacefully perched on the front of Café Hon for 7 years until City officials categorized the sculpture as a sign and levied an $800 annual fee against it. Denise decided to take it down in protest and the public joined forces with her. During the City Hall rally, Mayor Dixon (top) autographed pink flamingos for charity while Denise addressed the media (following page). The city agreed to reduce the fee and placed a few Hampden road signs on Interstate 83 directing tourists to the neighborhood.

Best Hon 2009

THE RETURN OF BIG PINK

A public celebration was held on the sidewalk in front of Café Hon for the unveiling of the new and improved pink flamingo sculpture. Young and old alike, including Elvis, came out to join in the festivities. Café Hon handed out pink flamingo lawn ornaments and feather boas to spectators. After the unveiling, Denise glowed with pride (right).

ELVIS

ELVIS

THE NIGHT OF 100 ELVISES

When Denise invited her Hon friends to a night out with 100 Elvises, I had to wear something special. I gave up the blonde beehive for a night out as a red head because I heard Elvis was partial to them. I hand-painted Elvis's portrait on a window screen and wore it around my skirt. We gathered at Café Hon for dinner before heading to the enormous Lithuanian Hall in Baltimore City. There we partied like rock star Hons and mingled with celebrities, including my fav Duff Goldman of Charm City Cakes (following page bottom). As always, it was for a good cause benefiting the Johns Hopkins Children Center.

14 YEARS OF
AND OYSTERS
STILL ONLY
$5.00 PER
1/2 DOZ
16th
NIGHT OF 100
ELVISES
ALL
ACCESS

AIN'T NOTHIN' BUT A HOUND DOG

SEASONS GREETINGS

MIRACLE ON 34TH STREET

My official duty as Baltimore's Best Hon was to ride with Denise in the Mayor's Christmas Parade through Hampden. This parade, sponsored by community associations and businesses in Baltimore's Hampden and Medfield neighborhoods, was lined with 25,000 spectators along the 2.5 mile route. I was honored to participate in such a special event. After the procession we returned to Café Hon, and I enjoyed a big hug from Santa (left) and a photo request with two precious parade attendees (right). Later that evening, I strolled down 34th Street (preceding page) to witness the miracle that thousands of people come to see each year. One block of Hampden homeowners join together to create a spectacular holiday light display that can surely be seen from outer space.

HON
Best Hon 2009

BLIEVE, HON

OFF BROADWAY

When the musical Hairspray was scheduled to perform at the Lyric Theater, I knew I had to be there. I was able to purchase great seats and treated my very favorite mother-daughter Hons, Rita and Heidi Moore, to a very special girls' night out. Both Rita and Heidi are former Baltimore's Best Hons and, in my eyes, are still the best Hons. We were invited backstage and posed with the cast for this amazing photograph.

TICKETS START AT $37
THE OPERA SHOW
OPERA WITH AN ATTITUDE!
"TOTALLY
APTIVATING!"
— THE DAILY EXPRESS
N SALE NOW!
STUDENT DISCOUNT AVAILABLE FOR $18.00
ANUARY 21 • 7:30PM
410-547-SEAT
www.ticketmaster.com
Audience Services 410-900-1150
THE LYRIC
LYRICOPERAHOUSE.COM
16-year-old Tracy Turnblad has a dream as big as her hair.
Can she get the guy and still have time to change the world?
BEST MUSICAL WINNER!
SEE IT LIVE!
8 TONY AWARDS 2003
hairspr
BROADWAY'S BIG FAT MUSICAL COMEDY HIT
JANUARY 8-9, 201

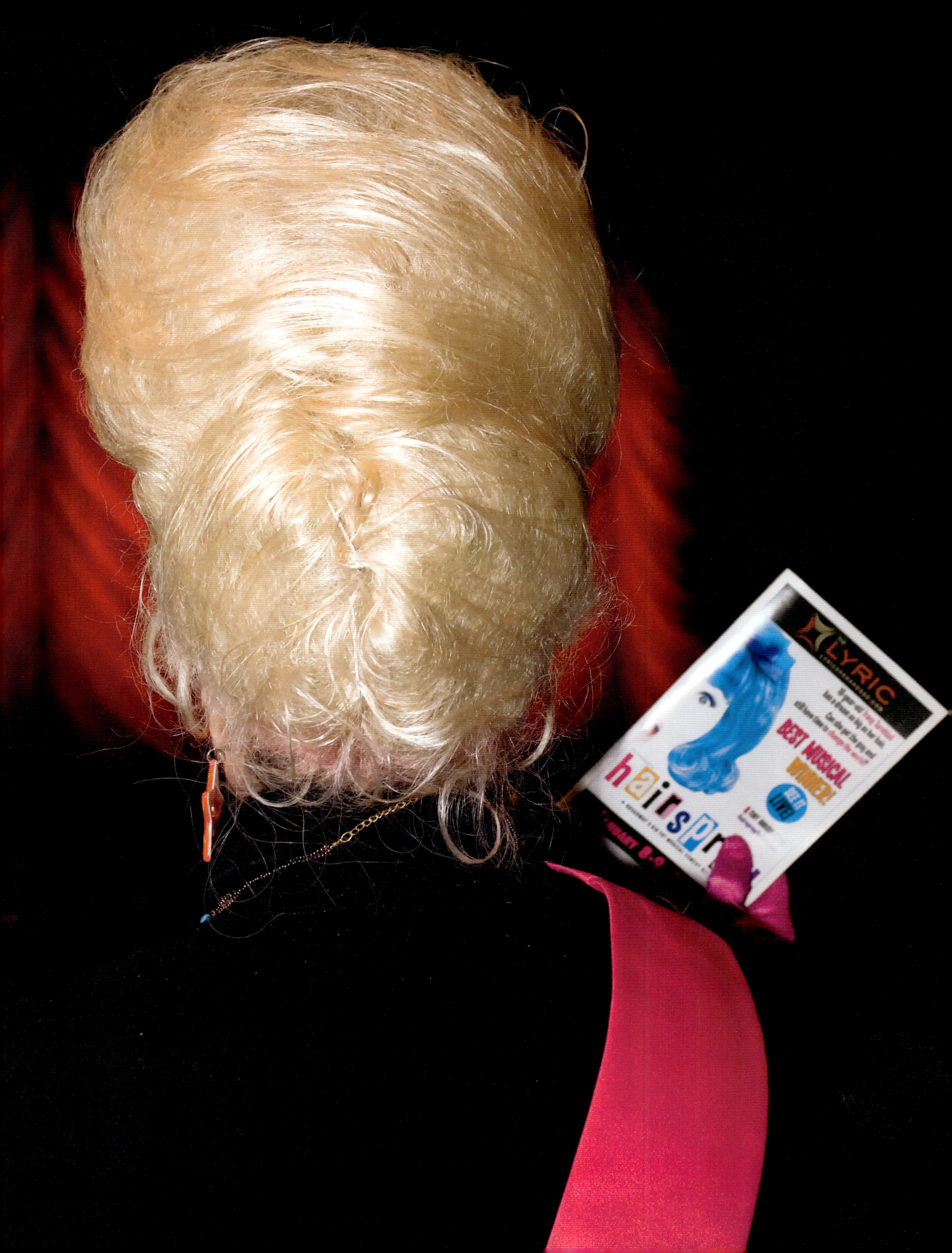
LYRIC
BEST MUSICAL
WINNER!
SEE IT
LIVE!
hairspr

HON FUN FUND RAISER

I jumped at the opportunity when The Beach House dock bar and restaurant in Dundalk invited me to guest Hontend at their rockin' benefit for Special Olympics Polar Bear Plunge. Plunge team The Mother Plungers (below right) joined in the fundraising activities. When Chris Burns (top right) and his band The Headshakes took the stage, I shook my hive on the dance floor and even found time to try my hand at a game of pool all before the stroke of midnight.

MYERS'S RUMS
HON

THE BEACH HOUSE
HON

THE PLUNGING HONS

The 14th Annual Maryland State Police Polar Bear Plunge lived up to its name. Freezing temperatures and heavy snow did not deter the determined from plunging into the icy wooder of the Chesapeake Bay. Denise Whiting gave me words of encouragement before I took the stage in the Miss Hypothermic Hon contest. I lost the contest but cheered up and warmed up quickly when super plunger Joe Flacco (below) walked by.

Following page: Heidi, Rita and Denise took the plunge in 2008.

SWEET TREATS

One visit to Shallow Creek Bookstore & Café (left) in Edgemere, Maryland, and I was hooked! Great books, delicious food, hand dipped ice cream and even an open mic night! This rare combination of offerings makes a perfect gathering spot for the community. I still race like a redheaded rabbit to Café HON for their carrot cake.

HEIDI & RITA

Rita, also known as The Queen Mother Hon, is royalty among the Baltimore's Best Hon winners. She is a Highlandtown native who lived in a rowhouse with her parents, seven siblings, grandmother and whoever else needed a place to stay. Rita has never had formal training as a Hon, but considers her upbringing in southeast Baltimore City to be a natural influence. Rita uses her training in cosmetology from Mergenthaler Vocational-Technical High school to sculpt skyscraper-high beehives for herself and her daughter. Rita revolutionized the Hon scene by wearing her housecoat and curlers out in public to Honfest, sparking dozens of people to tell her that she reminded them of their (insert relative name here). She can often be seen sharing her Old Bay seasoning to help others "spice up their lives," and eating steamed crabs with family and friends.

Rita is the mother of another Baltimore's Best Hon winner, Heidi, who made her mother proud by winning the contest following her mother in 2004. Despite witnessing her daughter walk across several college graduation stages, she proclaimed that this was "the proudest a mother could be."

Her home in Middle River reflects her love of Hon style and can easily be spotted by the pink flamingos which decorate her front lawn. Rita enjoys gardening, being a grandmother and actively refusing to grow old gracefully.

Heidi was born and raised in southeast Baltimore City, Highlandtown to be exact. She grew up scrubbing marble steps for quarters and spending all of her free time in Patterson Park with her two younger brothers. She comes from a long line of Baltimore Hons, including her Great Aunts, Rita and Lorraine, Grandmother Ethel, and of course her mother Rita.

Heidi knew nothing of the world that existed outside of her neighborhood and assumed that everyone wore housecoats, went to the grocery store with their hair in curlers, religiously went to Bingo, and spoke with an unusual pronunciation of 'o.' After attending college in exotic Baltimore County, realizing that a Hon was not found anywhere else, and that it was truly an honor to have spent such time amongst a Baltimore treasure, Heidi talked her mother into attending their first Honfest in 2003. As Heidi described it to her mother, "There's this contest where people dress up and act like you and the ladies from the neighborhood. You can't lose." Proving her words to be more than true, Rita won the honor of Baltimore's Best Hon, wearing her finest housecoat. Heidi earned the title of Baltimore's Best Hon, in 2004, succeeding her mother by playing "Take me out to the Ballgame" on her homemade Natty Boh xylophone in front of a cheering crowd. Since then, they have attended Honfest annually and try to bring the Hon spirit to Baltimore events, such as the Baltimore Marathon and the Polar Bear Plunge.

Heidi resides in eastern Baltimore County with her wonderfully supportive fiancé Dante, and their two dogs Kasey and Hon (of course).

14th Annual
MSP POLAR BEAR PLUNGE
MARYLAND STATE POLICE
PBP
POLAR BEAR PLUNGE

SUPER BOWL HON-DAY

While the men were off to worship the gods of football, my girlfriends and I joined Elvis in the Hon Cave (female version of a man cave) to celebrate Super Bowl HON-day. We enjoyed my special recipe of Hon-tinis which include pink and blue passion fruit flavored vodkas over mini beehives of cotton-candy in a martini glass.

Swine Flu
Survivor

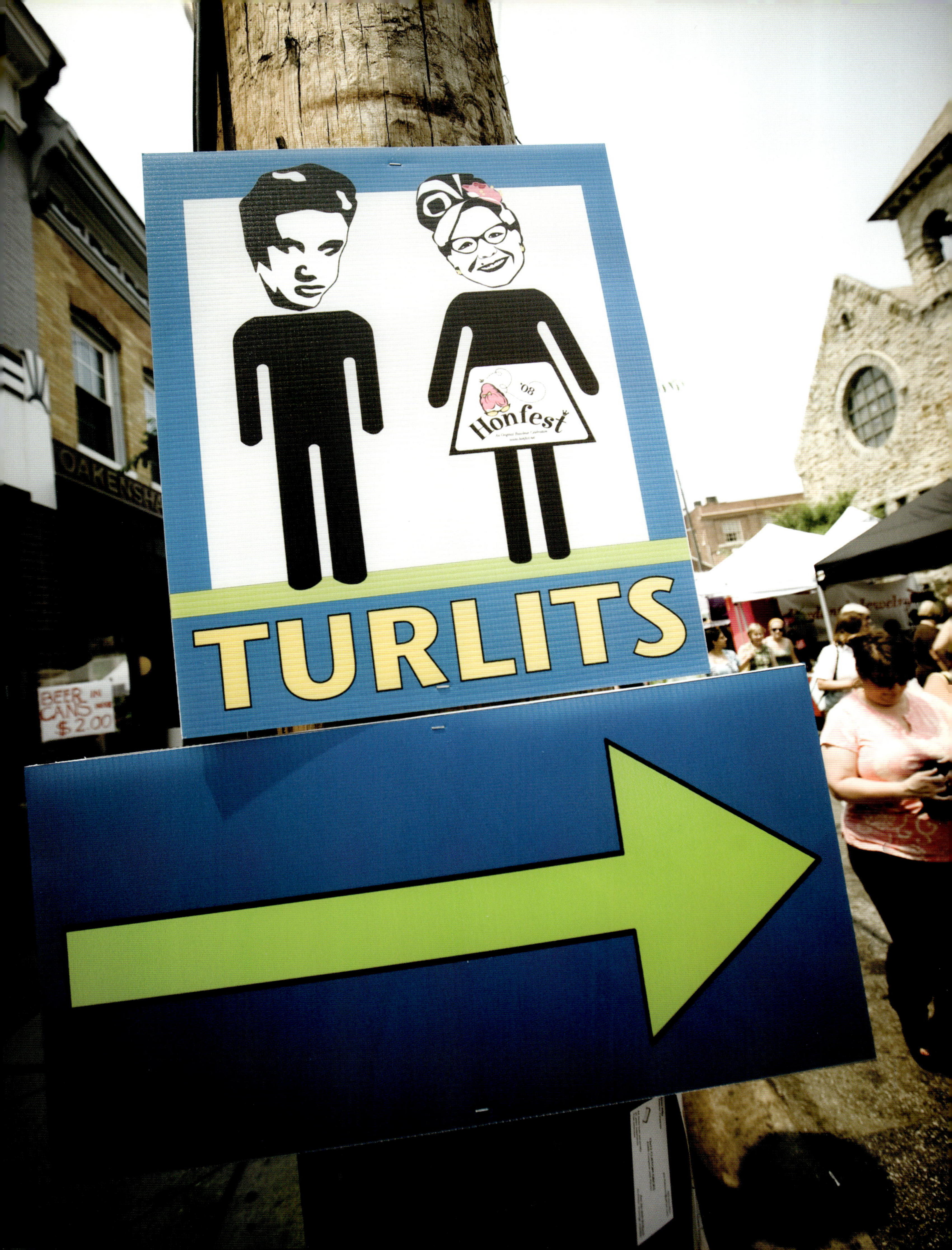
'08
Honfest
TURLITS
BEER IN
CANS
$2.00

BE MY VALENTINE

February 14th was a very memorable day, not because of candy and flowers but because of the special residents and staff of Riverview Rehabilitation and Health Center in Essex, Maryland. My dear Uncle Franklin Osborne (lower right) who had been a recent patient at Riverview was delighted when I suggested we return for a visit. We were joined by my best Hon Heidi Moore and professional Elvis impersonator Tommy El of DB Entertainment. The residents and staff gathered in the main dining room. My uncle presented them with flowers while Elvis had them enjoying youthful memories with his songs.

Riverview
HABILITATION & HEALTH CENTER

Valentine's Day
BaWlmer Hon's
Performance
February 14, 2010
2:30pm
In the Crane Dining Room
Don't Miss It!!!
LOVE
LOVE
S.W.A.K

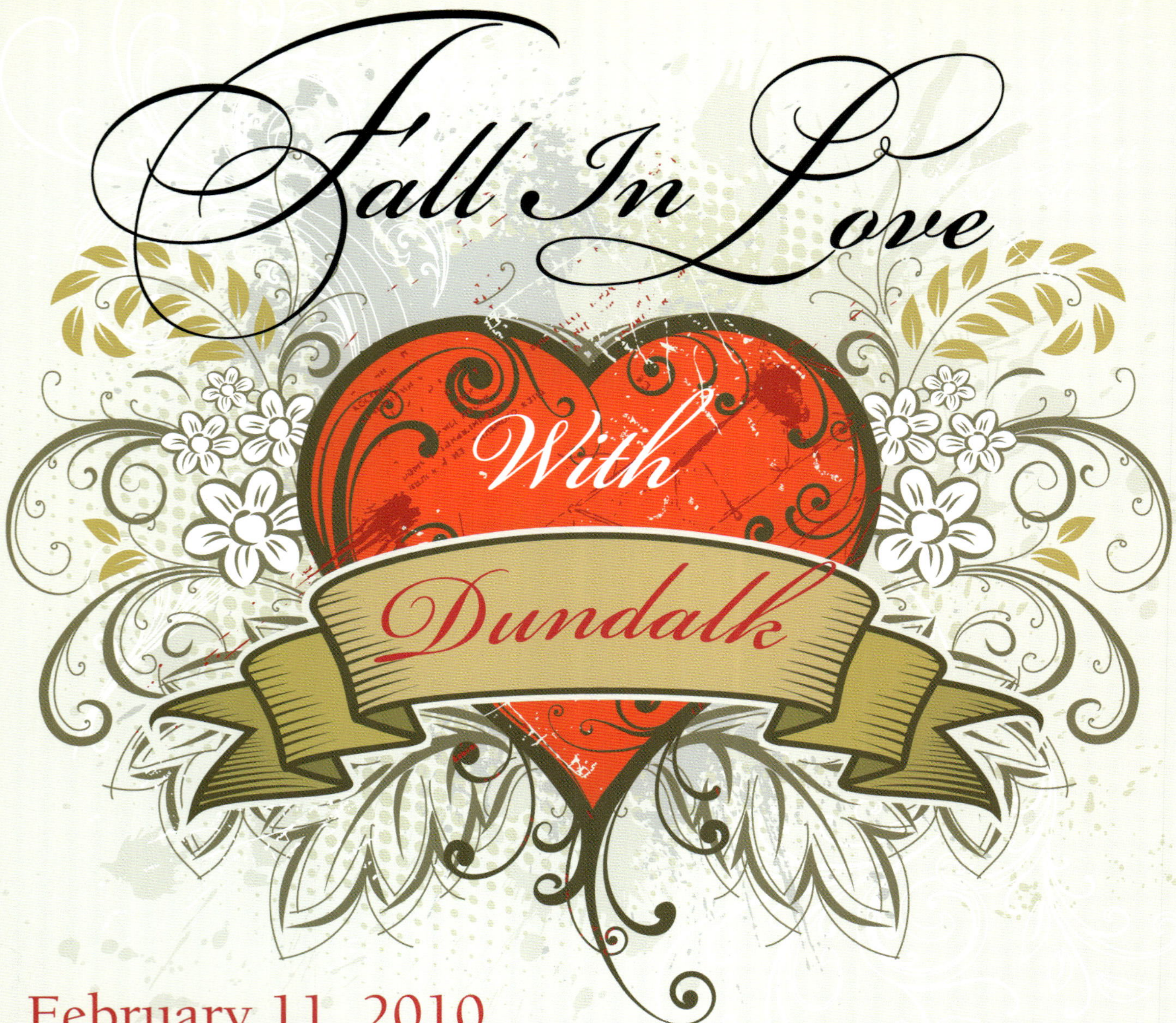

Fall In Love With Dundalk

February 11, 2010
5pm – 7pm

2 Dunmanway (Second floor)
Dundalk, Maryland 21222

RSVP 410-282-0261
Snow date: February 18, 2010

Big City access – Small Town feel

Presented by Dundalk Renaissance Corp in partnership with JMJ Properties

11Center Place, Dundalk, Maryland 21222
www.dundalkusa.org

You are cordially invited to a professional networking event to promote Dundalk Main Street and all it has to offer businesses.

♥ Tour reasonably priced newly renovated commercial rentals with historic charm and visual appeal.

♥ Get business resources that will assist you with growing your business.

♥ Enjoy the opportunity to meet and greet other entrepreneurs.

♥ Refreshments served

♥ Bring your business Cards to enter drawings for gifts and prizes

HOMETOWN GIRL

I was honored when Main Street Manager for the Dundalk Renaissance Corporation, Jennifer Funn (below left) invited me to attend a professional networking event. It was a privilege to be in the company of so many dedicated community leaders and business owners, including Dundalk's Citizen of the Year the charismatic Mr. Dennis McCartney (below center).

Utz
CHARM CITY CAKES
My
Big Fat
Bawlmer Wedding
SAVE THE DATE!
Friday, February 26, 2010
UAW Hall – Brewer's Hill
1010 S. Oldham Street
Baltimore, MD 21224
Come in your most Outrageous Wedding Attire!
The Wedding Event of 2010 Surprises:
Wedding Menu:
Hot Roast Beef;
Mashed Potatoes;
Green Beans/Corn;
Featuring Live Mus
by SLC

AMP IT UP, HON

Always ready to chicken dance for a good cause, I was joined on the floor by members of the Art & Music Project of Baltimore. AMP, a non-profit organization devoted to social change through the healing powers of art, culture and music, called upon me to perform the apron dance at My Big Fat Bawlmer Wedding. Many of the guests donned wedding attire for this fun event, including a duct tape bridesmaid dress with a Natty Boh decal. Priceless! Many Baltimore businesses (left) donated to this important cause, including a generous gift certificate from Charm City Cakes.

W
T
99
SET
DISP
SCN

Bawlmer's Best Hon 2009
STEVE
MARTIN
ALEC
BALDWIN
THE OSCARS
WATCH IT UNFOLD LIVE
SUNDAY MARCH 7TH 8ET/5PT
abc
OSCAR.COM

AND THE OSCAR GOES TO...

AIRS, whose invaluable efforts to enhance the quality of life for low-income and homeless individuals and families living with or at risk of HIV/AIDS or other disabilities, has made a difference in many lives. The 9th Annual Oscar Night Baltimore Gala, a fundraiser presented by AIRS, had me rubbing elbows with such dignitaries as the Honorable Stephanie Rawlings-Blake, Mayor of Baltimore, and Brooke Poklemba, Miss Maryland 2009.

AIRS committee member Randon Fritsch (far left)

YOU'VE NEVER SEEN OSCAR LIKE THIS
STEVE MARTIN
ALEC BALDWIN
THE OSCARS
WATCH IT UNFOLD LIVE
SUNDAY MARCH 7TH 8ET/5PT
abc
OSCAR.COM
Bawlmer's Best Hon 2009

Bawlmer's Best

IT TAKES A VILLAGE

Keeping a Hon on the run is no small feat. After months of guest appearances, including a black tie gala, two parades, and a sold out benefit rock concert, this Hon needed a little TLC. Okay, a lot of TLC. Like a NASCAR pit crew, I am supported by my self-appointed Hon Maintenance Team. Dr. Eric Williams (top) of Katzen Eye group keeps my cat-eyes in focus while Dr. Michael Martin (top right) of Adio Chiropractic keeps me and my attitude adjusted.

And then there are the feet ... no small feat to keep these dogs from barking. Dr. Max Weisfeld (below right) of Joppa Foot Care has what it takes, including an occasional scolding, and his lovely wife Fran (following page) to keep me in line.

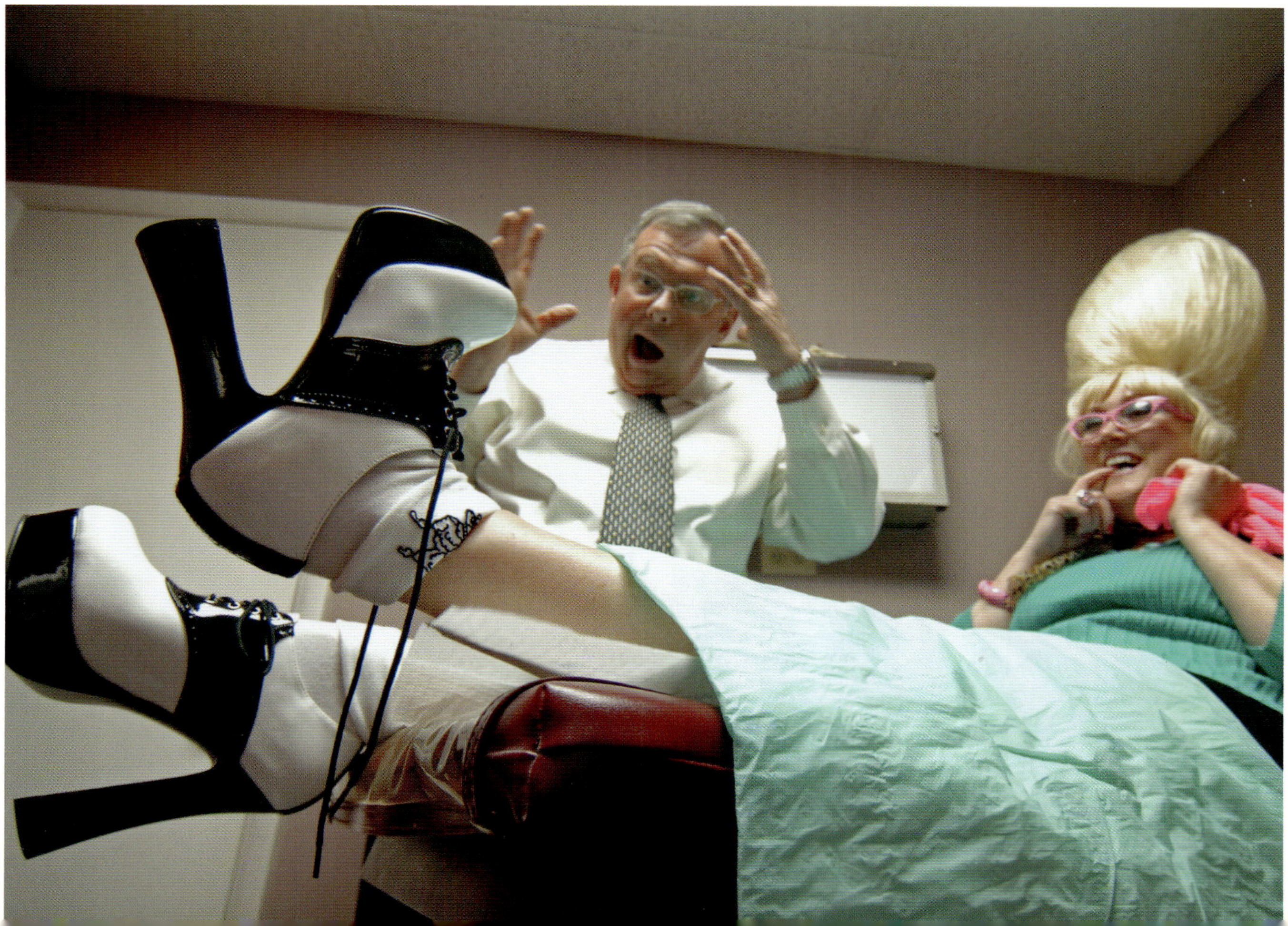

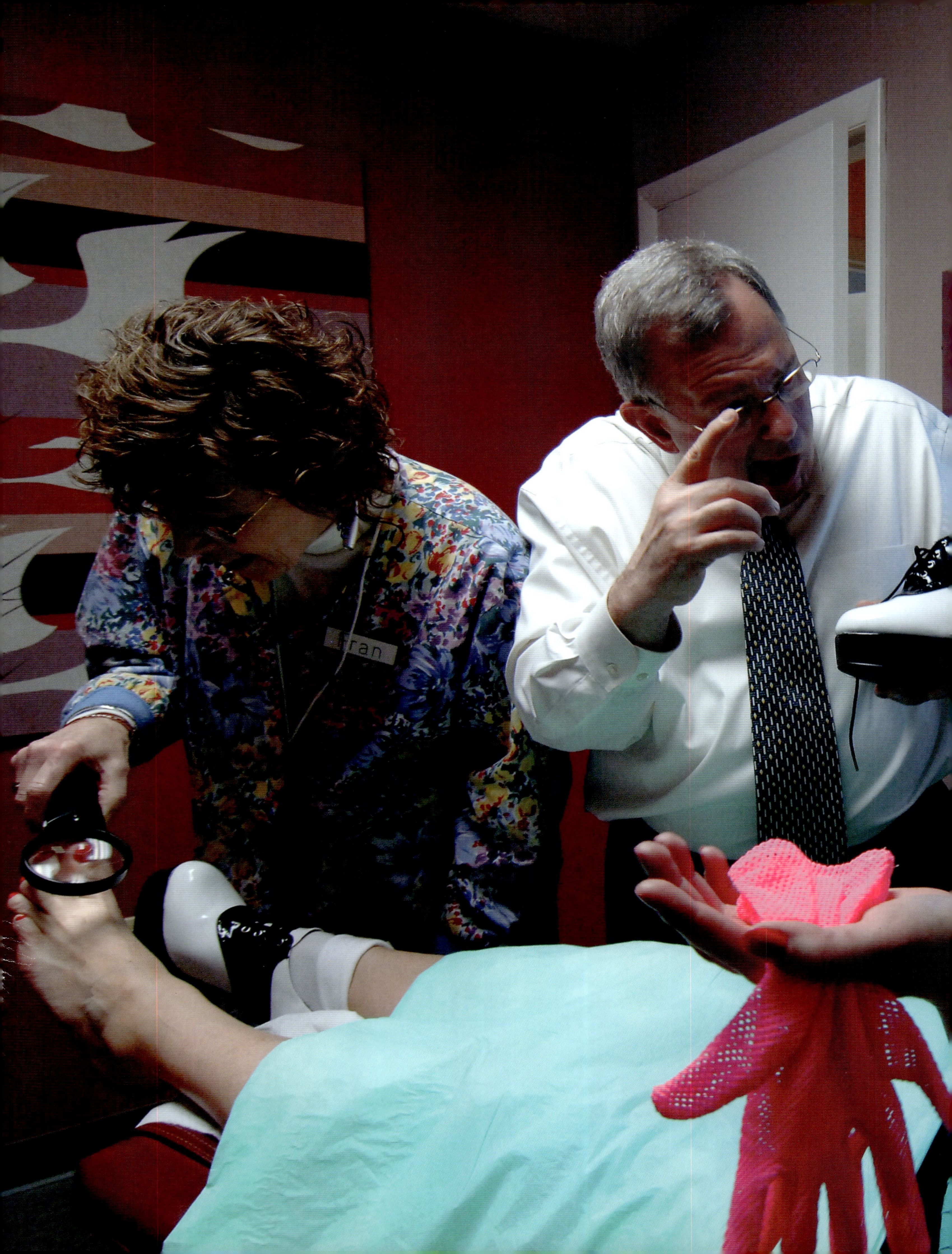
Fran

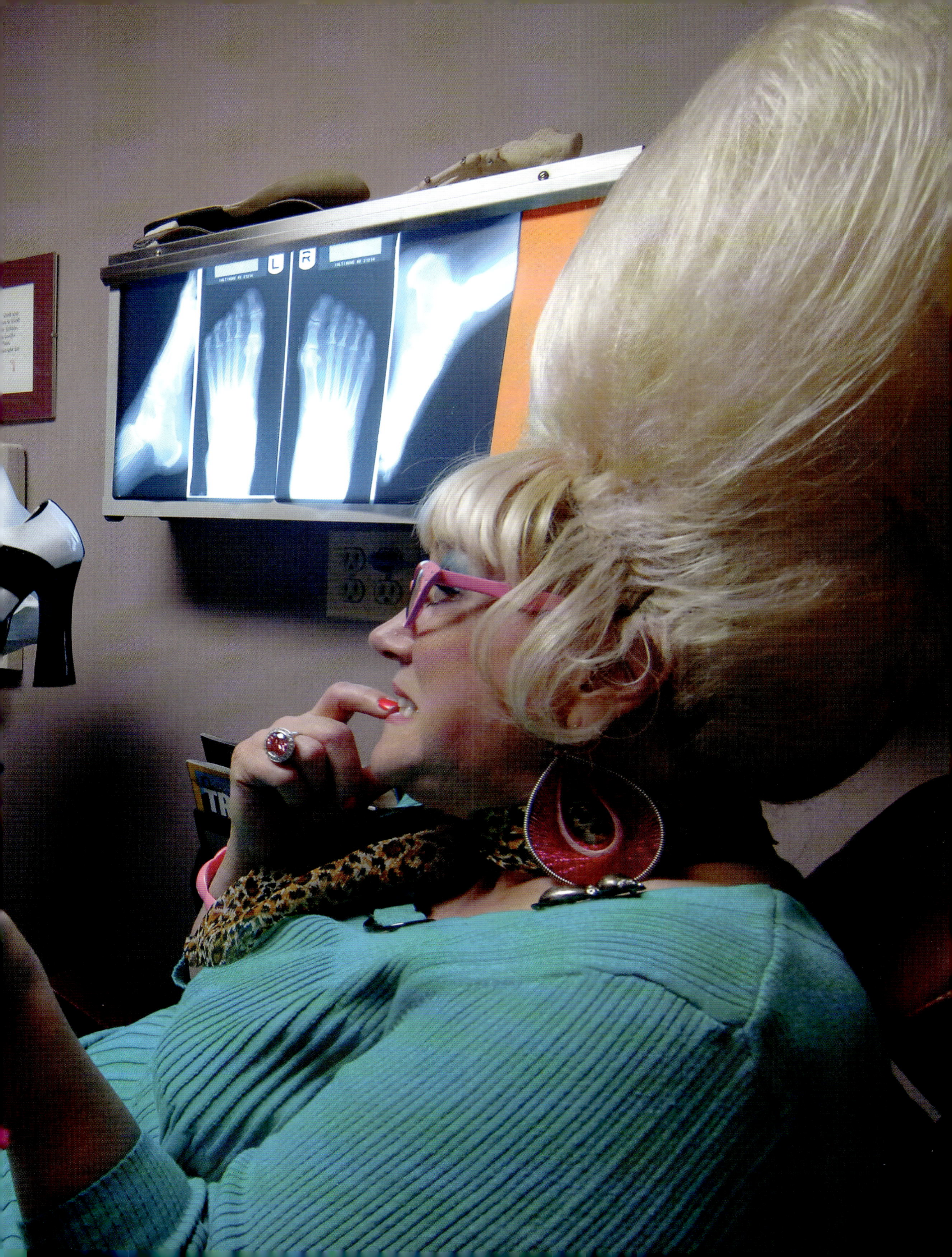

I
DUNDAL

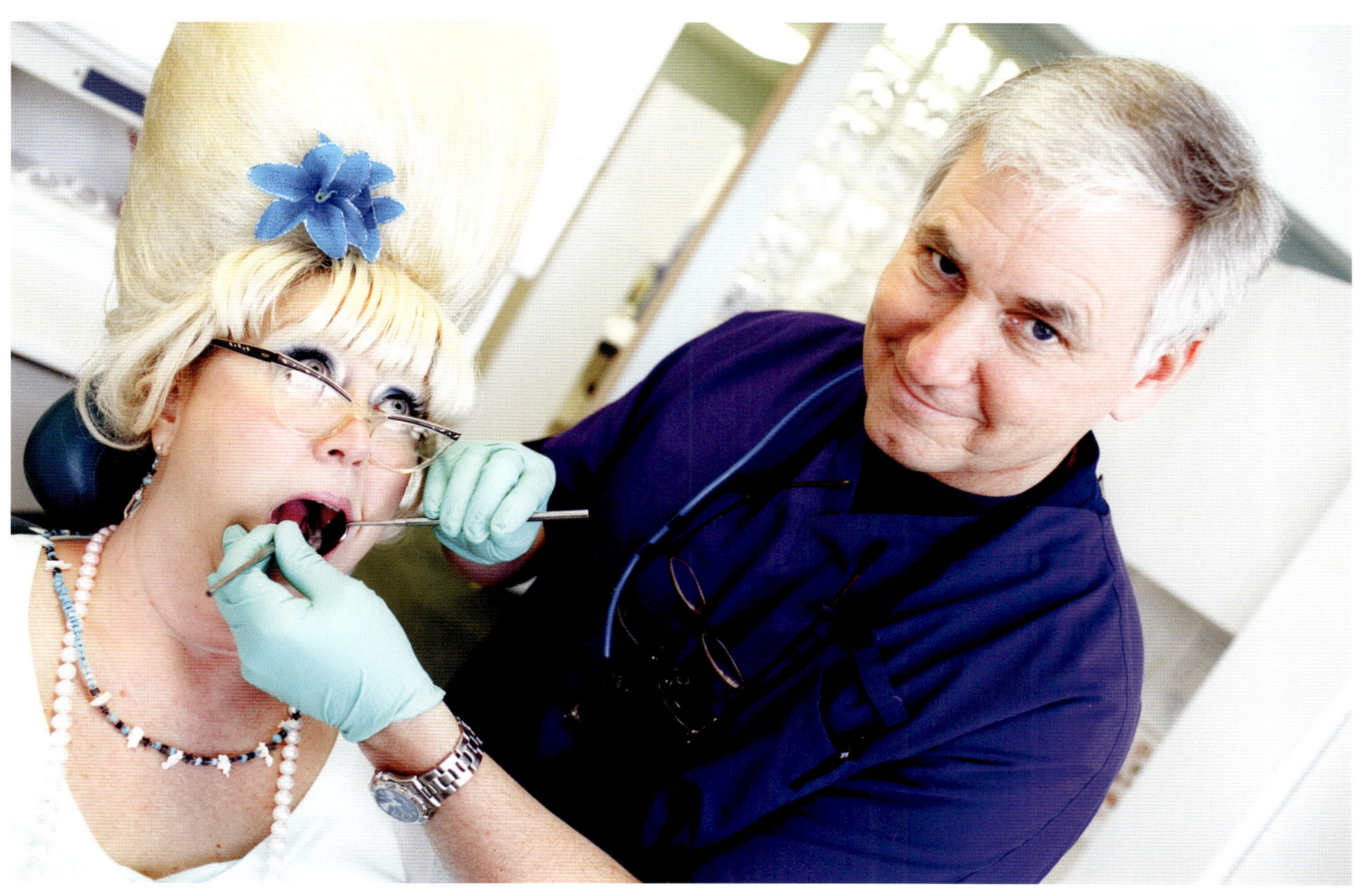

AND THEN SOME

My good friend and personal trainer, Lisa Lovejoy of Inside Out Fitness (left) encourages me to strengthen my core. I think she enjoys watching me sweat. She says it's healthy... for me or for her? If by now you are getting tired of seeing me smile you can blame it on Dr. John McCombe (top). He helps me keep my pearly whites white and has me grinning from ear to ear with his fun and relaxing manner.

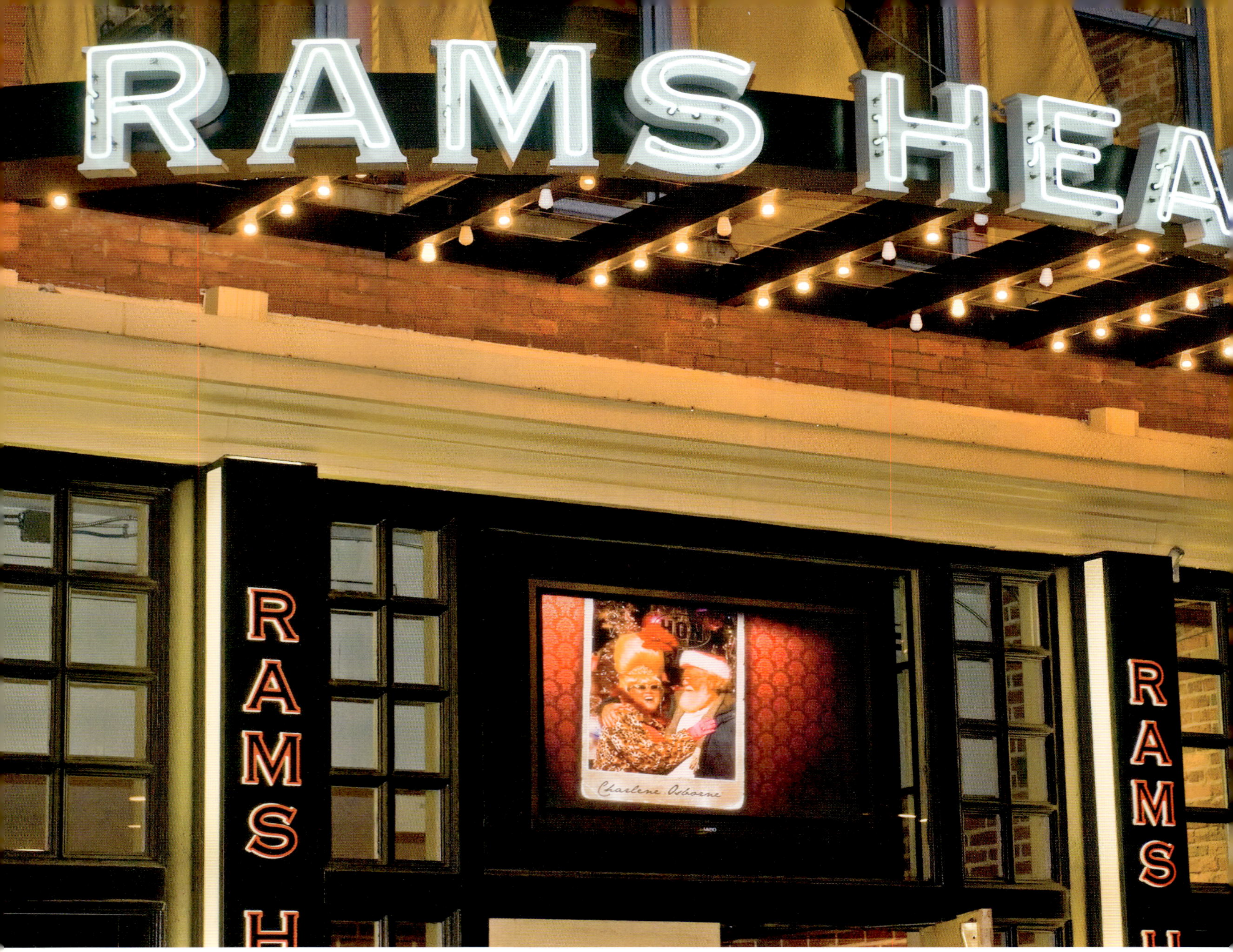

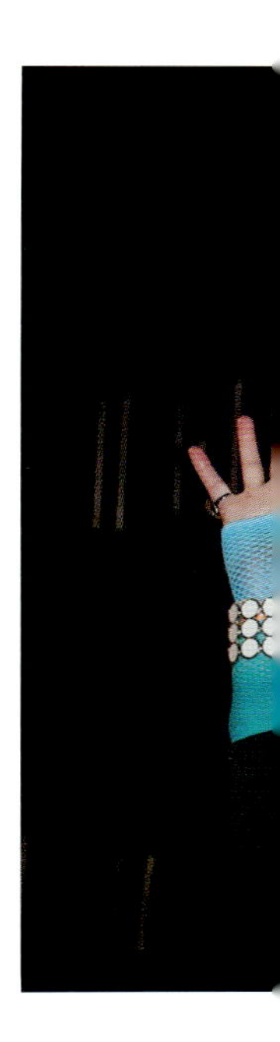

HAPPY 5TH ANNIVERSARY RHL

When Rams Head Live requested a Hon for their *All Things Baltimore 5th Anniversary Bash,* I jumped at the chance. I knew it would be a packed house when I heard the legendary KIX (following pages) would be headlining. With this, and my beehive in mind, I invited Baltimore's own, stunning six foot six, rock solid two hundred and seventy pound professional wrestling super star Mark *Van Hammer* Hildreth (below center) to escort me for the evening. The opportunity to raise money for *Cancer Sucks* and to appear on stage with 98 Rock's phenomenal Stash (right and far bottom left) was pure heart-pounding excitement. A night I will never forget.

Hon 2009

STAGE

LUCK OF THE IRISH

Too late, I missed the opportunity to register to walk in Baltimore's St. Patrick's Day parade. To my rescue came Bawlmer Craft Beers, the best new brewery in Baltimore with an invitation that saved the day. I was honored when Bawlmer Craft Beers owner, John O'Melia and family (page 123, bottom), welcomed me into their group. There were 105 groups in the line of march so you can imagine my surprise to see the Irish descendants of Dundalk's founding family on the McShane Bell Foundry float (above). All of Baltimore and Dundalk was green with Irish pride. Even the members of the Dundalk Renaissance Corp. (right) had the spirit.

Certificate of Recognition
Good Neighbor Week
DUN

ERIN GO BRAUGH

PAY TO PARK
NO PARKING

Best Hon 2009

DOWNEY OSHIN, HON

My HON-derful year would not be complete without a trip downey oshin, hon. Joined by best Hon friends Rita and Heidi Moore (left) we hit the beach and boardwalk for some good ole hon fun. When the Castle in the Sand Hotel got word the Baltimore Hons were coming, they rolled out the flamingo pink carpet and treated us like royalty. A trip to Ocean City would not be complete without an exciting round of miniature golf at Old Pro Golf, delicious Pizza Tugos pizza, and a spectacular Fager's Island sunset.

coconuts
BEACHFRONT RESTAURANT
BAR & GRILL

Castle in the Sand
HOTEL
BALTO HON OF
2009
watchFire SIGNS
NO VACANCY
AAA
Approved

HONS GO CLUBBING

PIZZA
TUGOS
OCEAN CITY
PIZZA
TUGOS
Galaxie 500

UGOS
SLICES
OPEN
Apparel
Entrance
Classic Taxi
410-289-1960's
Ocean City, MD

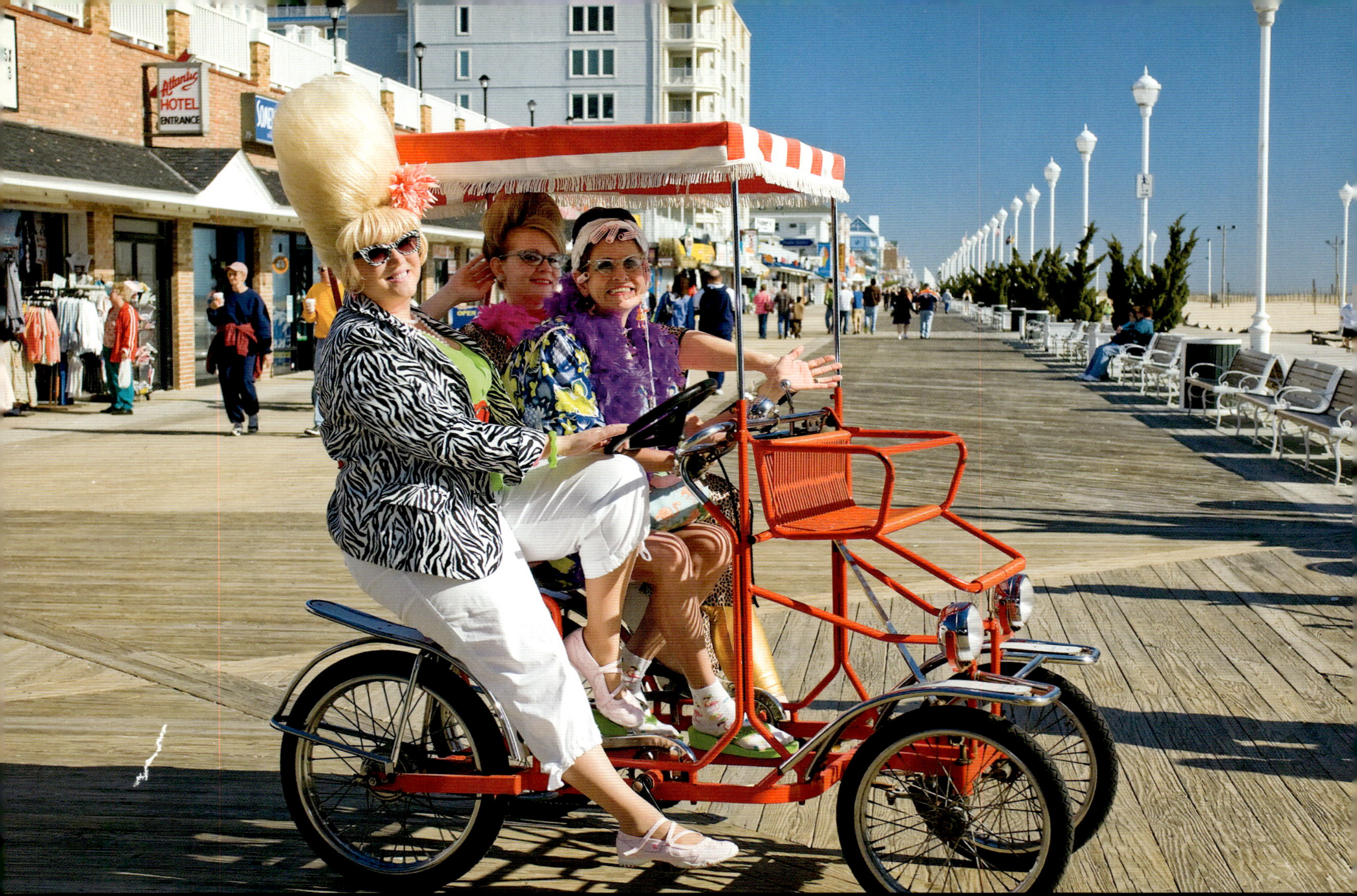
Atlantic
HOTEL
ENTRANCE

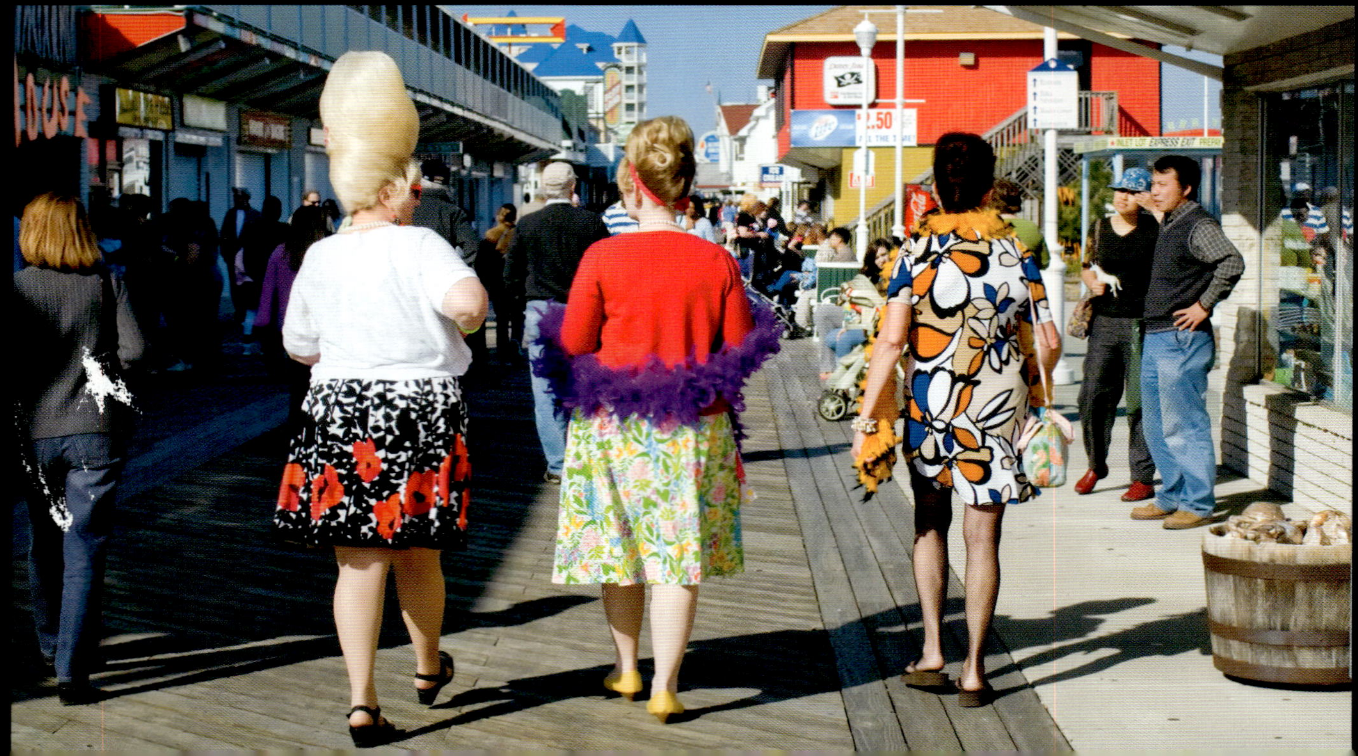

Coca-Cola

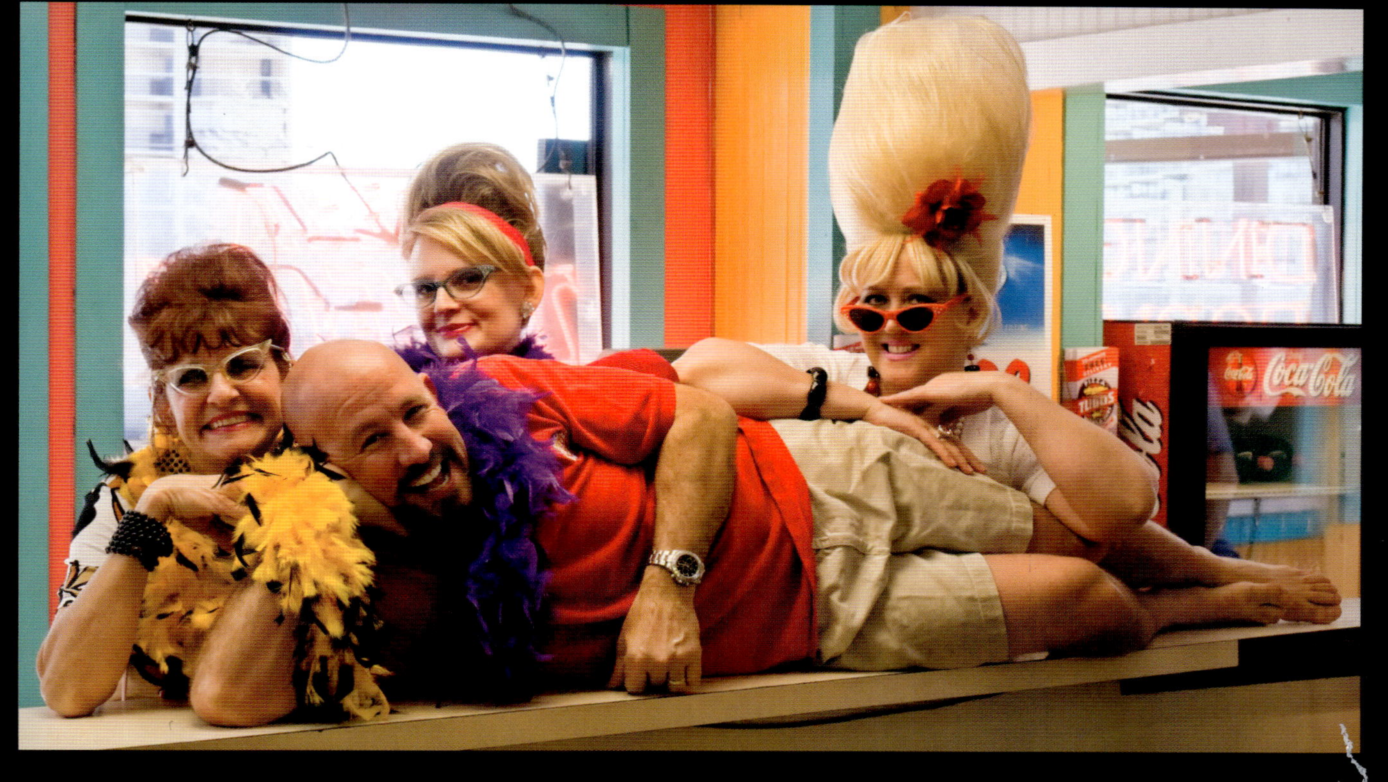

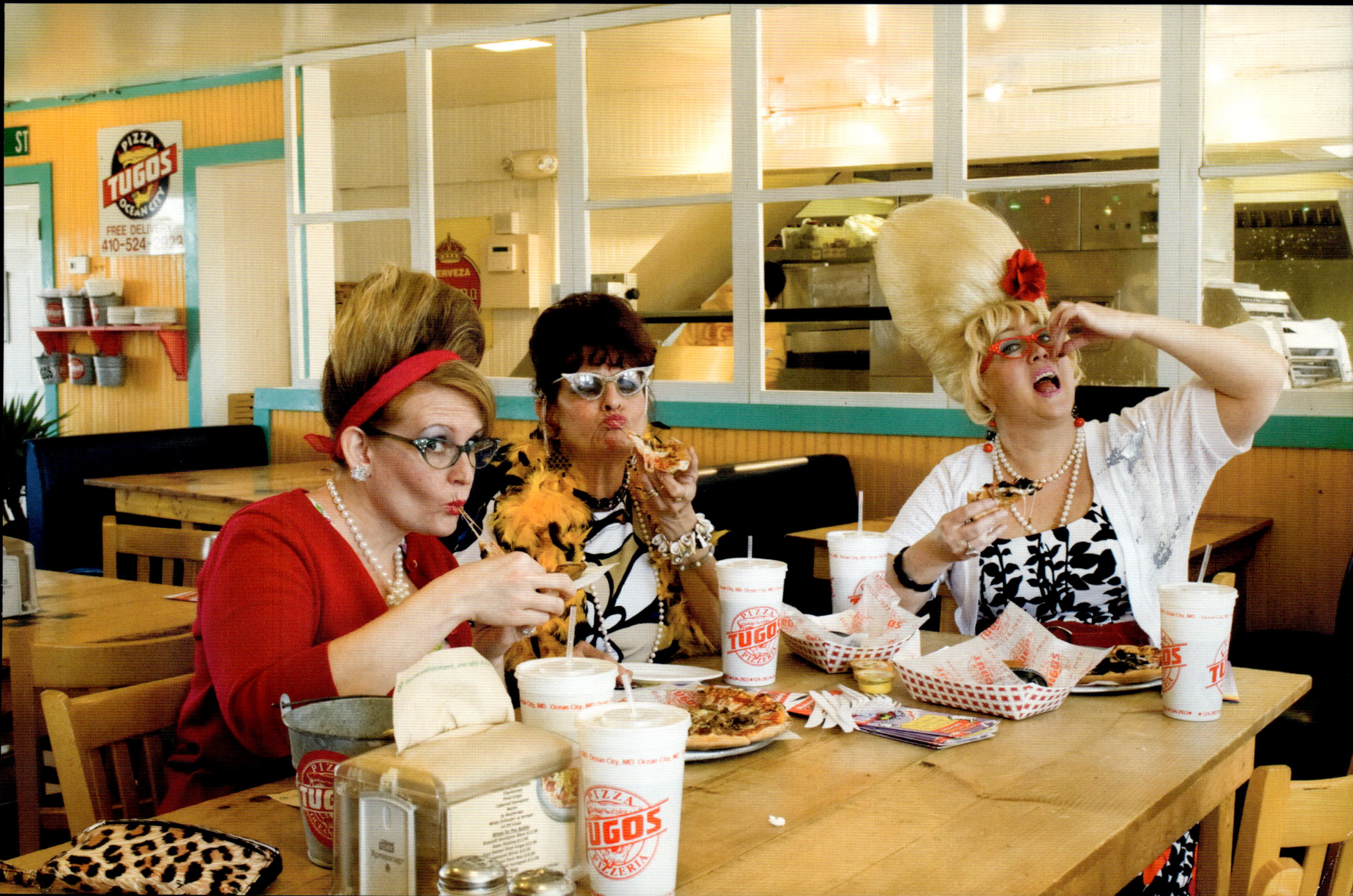
PIZZA
TUGOS
OCEAN CITY
FREE DELI
410-524-
PIZZA TUGOS PIZZERIA

David use

Principal tographer

After m years chasing books around dusty sh in public libraries, David Muse began a new career. His background in information science, his passion for sharing his work, and the personal rewards of helping others led him to freelance photography and teaching. Each year David conducts a number of popular photo tours, trips and workshops in and around Baltimore, MD and throughout the greater Mid-Atlantic region. He shows people where to find great images and how to capture them.

David is an avid writer. Maryland Life Magazine published his most recent article in their September/October 2009 issue -- on photographing the mountains of western Maryland during fall foliage season. On a regular basis he contributes how-to articles to Photographers Alliance Workshops (www.paworkshops.net).

Photographing My Year as Baltimore's BEST HON was a real hoot for David. Following Charlene and documenting her HON-derful reign was a fun-filled adventure. David said it was a rewarding experience to witness time and time again how pleased and happy people were to meet Charlene and her character. Both the young and the young-at-heart would smile and, often with a twinkle in their eye, ask for a photo with Charlene.

David is already busy at work on his next book project... a photographer's guide to Maryland.

Find full information about photo tours & workshops at www.baltimorephotosafari.com.

www.davidmusephoto.com
Email: davidm.muse@gmail.com
Cell: 443-812-5028

Jaime Windon

Contributing Photographer

I take pictures and I tell stories. Life couldn't be better and I can't imagine doing anything else.

Truth be told, I'm head over heels in love with the world and its people. Documenting life is a privilege and an honor, and a challenge I am thrilled to take on.

I am driven by the desire to capture true personality, intense emotion, inspiring love, and the fleeting moments that make up our lives. My specialty is documentary lifestyle photography and my ideal subjects are people who are in love with life, with each other, and with the world around them.

I have had the privilege of traveling to many awe-inspiring countries on many different continents, and observing life as it unfolds in various cultures. I've called many places home, from the east coast of the United States to the west, from the bustling streets of London to the remote regions of the Amazon – and I loved them all.

When I'm not shooting pictures or writing stories, I find great satisfaction in volunteering with organizations that I believe in. Educational initiatives and programs that inspire and motivate individuals are closest to my heart. I believe strongly in education, art, and communication: through these three efforts I am convinced we can change and shape our world for the better.

I also believe in love at first sight, that candid photography is an art form, and that I can change the world.
www.theblondephotographer.c n

Middleton Evans

Contributing Photographer, Layout Editor

Middleton Evans believes that beautiful photographs are nourishment for the soul, connecting us to God in mystical ways. His lens seeks the essence of the Divine in his wide-ranging subjects, as all created beings and works of art ultimately bare the signature of the Creator. Much of his 20-year career has been devoted to documenting the many faces of Maryland, including Chesapeake Bay watermen, cities and towns, festivals, farm life and equestrian sports. Wildlife photography has become a keen interest, especially our feathered friends that rule the sky. Evans' self-published books include Maryland in Focus, Baltimore, Maryland's Great Outdoors, Bodhi: The All American Lodge Dog, and Rhapsody in Blue: A Celebration of Nor' American Waterbirds. A book on the natural treasures of Baltimore's Patterson Park is in the works. Since 2000, Middleton has also published the Maryland: America in Miniature wall calendar series, featuring the state's diverse cultural and natural scenery.

Blessings to all!
www.ravenwoodpress.com

ACKNOWLEDGEMENTS

I thank God for letting me live my best life. ☙ Denise Whiting for creating HonFest and inspiring me to be the Best Hon that I could be. ☙ David Muse for your hard work, commitment, talent and friendship. You believed in me enough to take a chance and you were brave enough to follow me on this journey. I will always be grateful for your herculean contributions in the making of this book. I hope to continue to be your muse. ☙ David & Kitty Muse for making me feel like family. ☙ Jaime Windon for your pure talent and heart. You are a ray of light. ☙ Middleton Evans for the generous gift of your time, talent, experience, and smile. ☙ Elizabeth Davidson for your professionalism, patience, and hard work. ☙ Caroline Davidson for being a cutie patootie ☙ Heidi Moore for your friendship from the first moment we met at HonFest. I will never forget your kindness and sweet sense of Hon style. You are the Best Hon ever! ☙ Rita Moore for taking me under your wing and teaching me the finer and funnier points of Hon life. You will always be a Best Hon and the only Best Queen Mother Hon. ☙ Master window screen painter Tom Lipka for sharing your talent. ☙ Jenny Campbell for sharing your painted window screen and fashion clothing talent. ☙ My dear Uncle Franklin Osborne for everything you do - you are an angel. ☙ Leon Kriebel for letting me keep my day job. You are the undisputed Best Boss, hon. ☙ Dr. Max Weisfeld and Fran Weisfeld for your genuine enthusiasm. You gave me the courage to stick my beehive out to explore & create the Hon-derful opportunities that I experienced this year including the creation of this book. ☙ John Waters for giving us so much to enjoy and build upon. ☙ Pat Moran for including me in your talent pool even though I'm just a small fish. ☙ Matthew Weiner for the award winning Mad Men. ☙ My WBCM family - thank you f[illegible] during all my Hon shenanigans. ☙ The Castle in the Sands Hotel for your heart-war[illegible]eption and generosity. ☙ Scott Heise (page 135 top) for being such a great host an[illegible]e cutie patootie. ☙ Tommy El of DB Entertainment - Thank you for your ch[illegible]d talented performances. ☙ About Faces Day Spa and Salon for your generos[illegible] Ivchankova for your magical make-up artistry. ☙ Giella for the Blaze Cha[illegible]on created for the Baltimore Hon. ☙ Jimmie Ward for your unconditiona[illegible] friendship - you have the patience of a saint. ☙ Gary and Kathy Grief for [illegible]ughtful friendship. My Dad thanks you too. ☙ Jennifer Funn for your friendship and supp[illegible] ☙ Taylor Smith-Clarke (page 31 & 123 center) for inspiri[illegible] me to be a better Hon. You are the most talented 11 year-old young lady I have ever met[illegible] forward to watching your career in the performing arts continue to blossom. ☙ Tatiana Guliano (page 84 right) for your talent, being the prettiest in pink and a real cutie. ☙ Blaze Starr for your inspiration and Bennie for your help. ☙ Bowie & Jense[illegible] Craig Spencer, Jeff Spies, Dave Johnson, Randon Fritsch, Melisa Keimig for your [illegible] support ☙ Lady Gaga for burning up my ear-buds before each event. ☙ [illegible]iring me to live my best life. ☙ Everyone I contacted on how to make this b[illegible]yone who said it can't be done. ☙ Everyone appearing in this book, you are beau[illegible]l and very special people who enjoy life to its fullest. ☙ Everyone who gave me a Hey Hon, a hon hug or just a hon smile, you have all touched my life in a hon-derful way and I will always be grateful.

God Bless

PHOTO CREDITS

Each photograph is listed by the number of the page on which it appears; followed, if necessary, by a letter indicating its position on the page. The letters follow a sequence from top to bottom.

David Muse
Page 3, 6-7, 15, 21b, 40, 42-43, 45-47, 54-65, 68-69, 71-81, 85, 88-89, 92-95, 97, 99-109, 116a, 117b-c, 118-119, 120a, 121-135, 140-141.

Jaime Windon
Page Front cover, 1, 20, 21a, 23a, 24, 26-33, 39, 44, 52-53, 70, 87, 90-91, 110-111, 139, 115a, Back cover.

Middleton Evans
Page 4-5, 38-39, 41, 66-67, 84, 110-115.

Other artists and photographers

Baltimore Sun Media Group, page 2, 48, 50

Leslie Bertram, page 18-19

Mark L. Dennis, page 49, 51

Donald Ely, Baltimore Magazine
Bawlmer's Best Hon illustration, page 34

Joseph M. Giordano,
©2009 Dundalk Eagle Newspaper, page 36-37

Eric Shane Haase, page 116b, 117a

Mary Kate McKenna, page 82-83

Heidi Moore, page 136

Rediscover Baltimore County,
Designer on Call Program, page 96

Chuck Ritz , pac 23b

William A. Si hoto Shots, page 120b

James Smut tist; Carla Crisp &
Mary Wo ection, page 98

TO BE CONTINUED...